Cocos2d-x 3.0

Game Development Programming for iOS and Android

Gustavo E. Rangel

Cocos2d-x 3.0

Game Development Programming for iOS and Android

First published: October 2014

Published by Dragon Back Games

Brussels, Belgium

ISBN-13: 978-1499599558

ISBN-10: 1499599552

http://www.dragonbackgames.com/

Acknowledgments

Writing this book was only possible with the support of lots people that gave their contribution to make it happen.

I would like to give my thanks and appreciation to Kai Zhao, Lei Zhang, to all other folks that gave their support during the fund campaign.

I would like also to thanks to Kenney for providing the art for this game and to the whole Cocos2D-x team for their effort in providing such a good engine.

CONTENT

Introduction to Cocos2d-x

What is Cocos2d-x

Cocos2d-x is an open source cross platform game engine designed to build applications for different platforms such as iOS, Android, Windows Phone, Blackberry and many others. Developers can use C++, JavaScript and Lua to build their applications. The engine has proved to work; at least 25% of the mobile games developed in the world are powered by Cocos2d-x. The main advantage of this engine is that a single source code can be ported to several platforms with little effort.

The goal of this book is to teach you how to build a game using Cocos2d-x. You will learn progressively how to use the different features provided by the engine to put them together in a single application. Using Cocos2d-x by itself is not enough to develop a game; so additional information about the ecosystem associated to the engine is included.

This book contains 10 chapters with the following content,

- **Chapter 1 – Introduction to Cocos2d-x**, provides an introduction about Cocos2d-x, a description about the new features available in version 3.0 and also a description about the game book Tap a Plane
- **Chapter 2 – Getting Started with Cocos2d-x**, describes the procedure to configure the engine in the development environment
- **Chapter 3 – Toolset and Support**, presents about some useful tools that could be used to support the development of the game
- **Chapter 4 – Sprites and Effects**, describes the basis about sprites, actions, animations and effects in Cocos2d-x
- **Chapter 5 – Multiple Layers and Multiple Scenes**, shows how to include multiple layers and multiple scenes in the game. Also it explains the role of the Director to control the flow of the application

- **Chapter 6 – Game Loop and Events**, describes how to use the game scheduler and also how to handle the touches events.
- **Chapter 7 – Physic Engines**, is about how to include Box2D within your game. It explains how to merge the bodies with the sprites, how to move them and how to detect collisions between bodies.
- **Chapter 8 – Game Layout**, is how on build and include a layout for your game. It is explains also how to scroll across the map, and how to include parallax effect.
- **Chapter 9 – Sound Effects and Music**, presents how to include sound effects and music in the game and how to control them.
- **Chapter 10 – Saving Game Data**, explains how to save game data using user default data and SQLite3.

What is new in Cocos2d-x 3.0

Cocos2d-x 3.0 delivers lots of fixes and also a bunch of new features such as:

- Replaced Objective-C patters with C++ (C++11) patterns and best practices
- Improved Labels
- Improved renderer
- New Event Dispatcher
- Physics integration
- New UI objects
- JavaScript remote debugger
- Remote Console support
- Refactor Image - release memory in time and uniform the API of supported file format
- Automatically generated Lua bindings, add LuaJavaBridge and LuaObjcBridge
- Update on template containers
  - CCDictionary is replaced by cocos2d::Map<>, usage
  - CCArray is replaced by cocos2d::Vector<>, usage
  - CCBool, CCFLoat, CCDouble are replaced with cocos2d::Value, usage

- Included 3D extensions, now you can include 3D models on top of the 2D environment

A complete description about the new features is described in the Cocos2d-x 3.0 release note available in the Cocos2d-x website.

The Book Game – Tap a Plane

This book provides a game example to give a complete explanation about how Cocos2d-x works. The game is called **Tap a Plane**. This is side-scrolling game about a plane attempting to dodge a row of pikes throughout a cave. You can find more information of the game at **Games** section of the **Dragon Back Games** website (http://www.dragonbackgames.com/games.html).

Thanks Kenney for providing the art for the book game (http://kenney.nl/).

Game Resources and Community Forum

All the support material used in this book is freely available online at the Dragon Back Games GitHub repository (https://github.com/DragonBackGames).

Also, you can access the book's forum to have further discussion about how to use Cocos2d-x for your games (http://www.dragonbackgames.com/forum/).

Getting Started with Cocos2d-x

This chapter provides a description about how to configure Cocos2d-x for two development environments, Windows 7 and Mac OS X. There is a description about how to run the test application and finally how to create from scratch your first application.

Installing Cocos2d-x

The configuration of Cocos2d-x depends completely on the working environment and target platform that you are thinking to use to develop your games. This book sticks to Microsoft Windows 7 and Mac OS X 10.9 as working environment, and Android and iOS as target platform.

If you plan to distribute your application or add in-app products on the market, you need to enroll to the Apple Developer Program or Google Play Developer Console.

To install the framework, go to the Cocos2d-x website (http://www.cocos2d-x.org/download), download version 3.0 and uncompress the files somewhere in your computer. From now on, that location is referred as **COCOS2DX_ROOT**.

The following sub-sections explain detail description about the framework configuration. Choose the most appropriate depending on what you need.

Configuration for iOS and Mac OS X

The configuration of Cocos2d-x under Mac is quite straightforward. Download and install the latest version of Xcode (https://developer.apple.com/downloads/index.action). To configure the engine open a new **Terminal** window

1. Go to the **COCOS2DX_ROOT** directory and run **setup.py**
2. The script will automatically create the environmental variables that you need

Testing the Working Environment

Now we proceed to build and run the test project

1. On Xcode open the project **cocos2d_tests.xcodeproj** located under **COCOS2DX_ROOT/build**
2. Under Product->Scheme select **cpp-test iOS** or **cpp-test Mac**
3. Build and run the project

Once you run the application, you should see something like this,

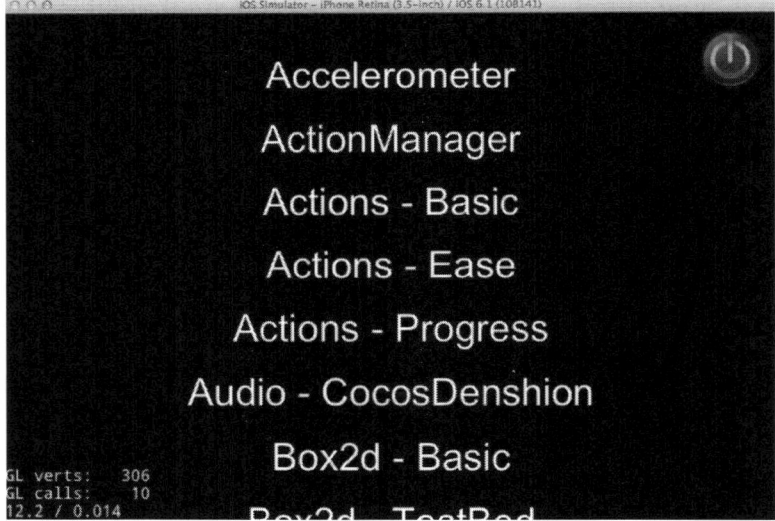

Configuration for Android on Mac OS X

The configuration of the Android development environment under Mac OS X requires the following tools:

- Java Runtime Environment, you can get it at the Java website (https://www.java.com/en/download/)
- Homebrew, with this tool you can install additional packages in your Mac (http://brew.sh/)
- Python, you can install this using Homebrew using `brew install python`
- Ant, you can install also this tool using `brew install ant`
- Android SDK, you can get the ADT bundle for Mac OSX at the Android Developer Website (https://developer.android.com/sdk/)
- Android NDK, this is a toolset that allows you to use C++ on top of Android. You can find the tool also at the Android Developer Website under the NDK section (https://developer.android.com/tools/sdk/ndk/)

To install the Android SDK and NDK you just need to uncompress the files somewhere in your computer. To configure your environment open a new **Terminal** window

1. Go to the **COCOS2DX_ROOT** directory and run **setup.py**
2. Indicate which is the location of the Android SDK, Android NDK and ant tool. The script will automatically create the environmental variables that you need
3. Open the file .profile under your user directory and add export `PATH=$PATH:$ANDROID_SDK_ROOT/tools:$ANDROID_SDK_ROOT /platform-tools`

Testing the Working Environment

Now we proceed to build and run the test project

1. Open a new **Terminal** window and go to the directory **COCOS2DX_ROOT/build**
2. Execute the command `python android-build.py -p 10 cpp-tests`

3. Connect your Android device via USB. Remember to enable **USB Debugging** on the device
4. Go to the directory **COCOS2DX_ROOT/tests/cpp-tests/proj.android/bin** and execute the command `adb install CppTests-debug.apk`

Once you run the application on your device, you should see something like this,

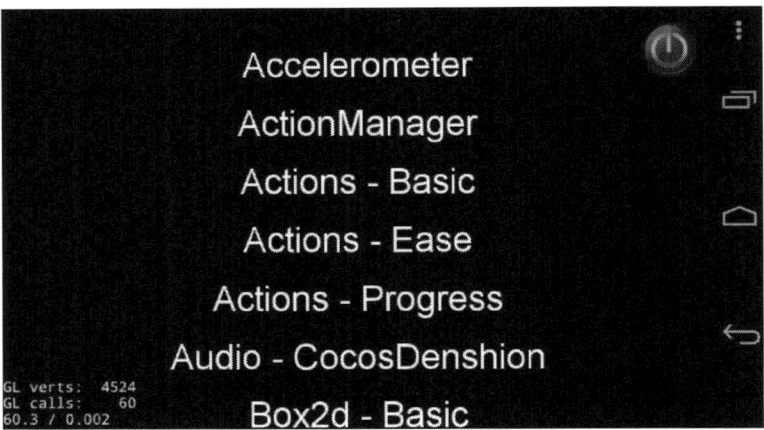

Configuration for Microsoft Windows 7

To use Cocos2d-x under Windows you need the following tools:

* Microsoft Visual Studio 2012, you can find the Express Edition at the Microsoft Download Center (http://www.microsoft.com/en-us/download/)
* Python 2.7, you can find it at the Python website (https://www.python.org/download/)

Testing the Working Environment

Once you download and install the tools, we proceed to build and to run the test project.

1. On Visual Studio 2012 open the solution **cocos2d-win32.vc2012** located under **COCOS2DX_ROOT/build**

2. Under the Solution Explore right click the **cpp-test** project and select Set as **StartUp Project**
3. Build and run the project

Once you run the application, you should see something like this,

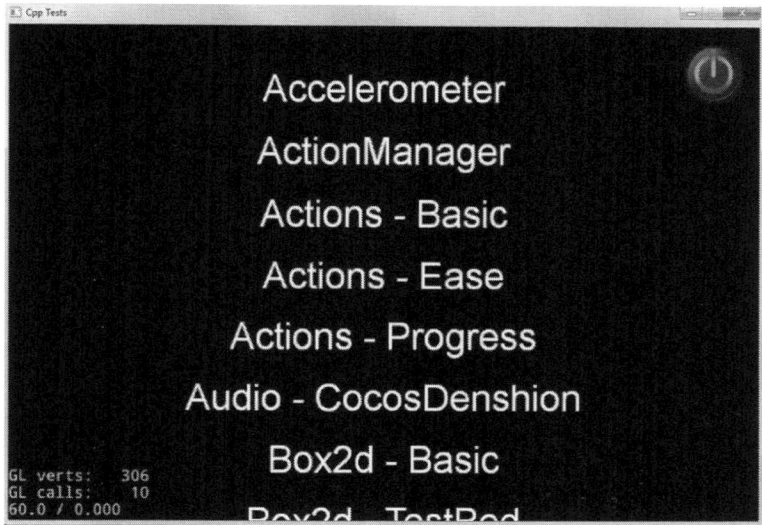

Configuring System Environment

Before creating a new project you should add the Cocos2d-x tools path into the system environment path.

1. Open the **Control Panel** and select **System**
2. Click on **Advance System Settings** and click on the **Environment Variables** button
3. Under the **System Variables** list create a new variable called **COCOS2DX_ROOT**, and as value put the directory where you installed the cocos2d-x
4. Under the **System Variables** list look for the variable **Path**, and at the end add **COCOS2DX_ROOT\tools\cocos2d-console\bin**. Do not forget to add a ';' as delimiter

5. Add also to the variable **Path** the location were Python is installed

Configuration for Android on Microsoft Windows 7

The configuration of the Android development environment under Windows 7 requires the following tools:

- Java Runtime Environment, you can get it at the Java website (https://www.java.com/en/download/)
- Cygwin, this tool emulates Unix environment on Windows. You need it to build the native code of your applications. Go to the Cygwin website and download version 1.7.x (http://cygwin.com/)
- Android SDK, you can get the ADT bundle for Windows at the Android Developer Website (https://developer.android.com/sdk/)
- Android NDK, this is a toolset that allows you to use C++ on top of Android. You can find the tool also at the Android Developer Website under the NDK section (https://developer.android.com/tools/sdk/ndk/)

Installing Cygwin

Once you download the **setup.exe** file continue with following steps to perform the installation:

1. Choose **Install from Internet**, then click **Next**, then choose the installation directory. You have to be sure that there are no spaces in the installation directory
2. Continue with the installation configuration, and once you reach the **Select Packages** look for the **Devel** branch and click once on top of it. You should see that from **Default** changes to **Install**
3. Click next and start the installation

Installing Android SDK and Android NDK

Just uncompress both Android files somewhere in your computer. Also, you need to be sure that there are no spaces in the installation directory. You need to create two environmental variables to define the location of the Android toolset

1. Open the **Control Panel** and select **System**
2. Click on **Advance System Settings** and click on the **Environment Variables** button
3. Under the **System Variables** list create a new variable called **ANDROID_SDK_ROOT**, and as value put the directory where you installed the Android SDK
4. Under the **System Variables** list create a new variable called **NDK_ROOT**, and as value put the directory where you installed the Android NDK
5. Under the **System Variables** list create a new variable called **JAVA_HOME**, and as value put the directory where you installed the Java Runtime Environment

Testing the Working Environment

Now we proceed to build and run the test project

1. Open **Cywin** and go to the directory **COCOS2DX_ROOT/build**
2. Execute the command `python android-build.py -p 10 cpp-tests`
3. Connect your Android device via USB. Remember to enable **USB Debugging** on the device
4. Go to the directory **COCOS2DX_ROOT/tests/cpp-tests/proj.android/bin** and execute the command `adb install CppTests-debug.apk`

Once you run the application on your device, you should see something like this,

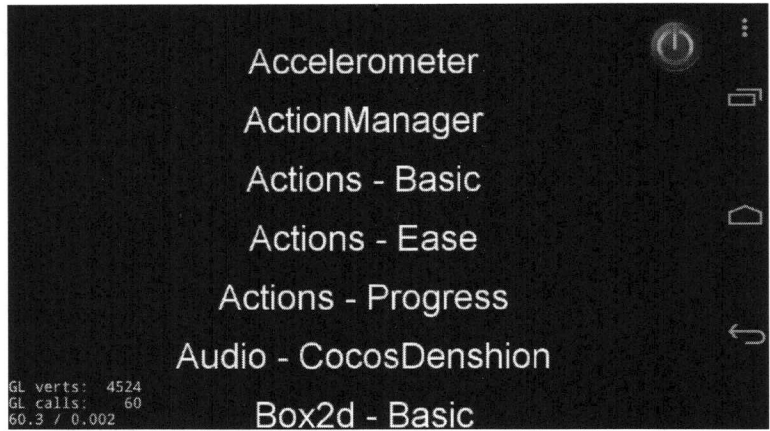

Creating a New Project

To create a new project, open a **terminal** or a **cmd** and use the following command line

```
cocos new PROJECT-NAME -p PACKAGE-NAME -l cpp -d PROJECT-DIR
```

Where,

- PROJECT-NAME is the name of your project
- PACKAGE-NAME is the package name for your project (e.g. com.edu.helloworld)
- PROJECT-DIR is the destination directory of your project

If you build and run the **HelloWorld** project you should see something like this

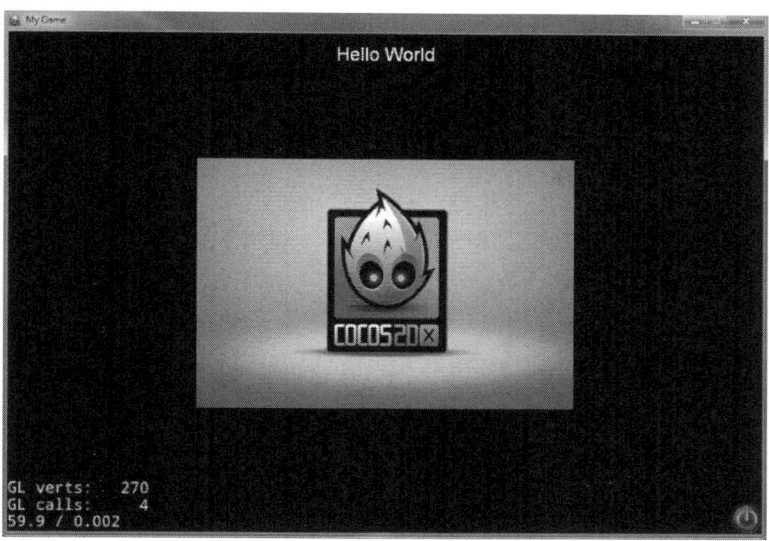

Summary

This chapter provided a complete description about how to configure Cocos2d-x on your working environment. Do not forget to run the test application. This will give you a complete overview about the features available in the engine.

Toolset and Support

This chapter is about the toolset available to support the development of your games. It describes several tools for each purpose, with more details in graphical tools, sprite sheets and physics, layout, animation, audio, and some additional utilities. The subsequence chapters provide a description on how in integrate these tools within Cocos2d-x.

Graphics Tools

There is a large amount of tools available in the market to create the graphics for your games. I will focus only some open source tools that I consider quite useful.

Gimp – GNU Image Manipulation Program

Gimp is a freely distributed piece of software for such tasks as photo retouching, image composition and image authoring (www.gimp.org)

Inkscape

Inkscape is a professional vector graphics editor for Windows, Mac OS X and Linux (http://www.inkscape.org/). The main reason why you want to use vector graphics for your game is resolution independence. You can scale your art without losing quality of your images and later exported to a png file.

Sprite Sheets and Physics

Sprite sheets allow you to arrange all the images for your games in a single file. In order to use this single file in your application you need a configuration file that defines the location of each image. The advantage of having all your images in a single file is that you can reduce the amount of number of calls at the rendering stage of your game.

Regarding the Physics, there are tools that allow you to define the physical shape of the body that represent a certain image. This will save you an incredible amount of time while developing games that make use of a physic engine.

TexturePacker

TexturePacker is a tool provided by **CodeAndWeb** that allows you to create sprite sheets in seconds (http://www.codeandweb.com/texturepacker). Basically, you just need to drag and drop all your images to the tool and publish the files that you need. You can also scale the sprite sheet to several resolutions without losing too much quality. There is another feature that becomes quite handy which is Content Protection. You can encrypt your assets to prevent that some stealth the content and use it somewhere else.

PhysicsEditor

PhysicsEditor is another tool provided by **CodeAndWeb** that allows you to create the collision shapes for your images in seconds (http://www.codeandweb.com/physicseditor). The tool provides a trace functionality that detects automatically the shape of the images. It allows you export a configuration file for several physics engine such as Box2d and Chipmunk.

ShoeBox

ShoeBox is a free Adobe Air based app for Windows and Mac OSX with game and ui related tools (www.shoebox.com.au/). With the tool you can create sprite sheets, read sprite sheets, generate bitmap fonts, extract tiles and many more. This is a free alternative for **TexturePacker**. However, this tool does not provides the automatic scaling nor the encryption protection.

SpriteHelper Pro

SpriteHelper Pro is a tool that allows you to create sprite sheets (http://www.gamedevhelper.com/spritehelper/). I would say that this tool is a combination of TexturePacker with PhysicEditor. There are additional features, such as animation editor, and including physic holes.

Audio

SFXR

SFXR is an open source tool that provides a simple means of getting sound effects for games (http://www.drpetter.se/project_sfxr.html). With the application the user can generate randomly effects that sound like typical actions such as jumping, shooting, hitting and others. There is a port for Mac OS X called CFXR (http://thirdcog.eu/apps/cfxr).

Audacity

Audacity is an open source tool for recording and editing sound effects (http://audacity.sourceforge.net/). The tool is available for both Windows and Mac OS

Layout

R.U.B.E.

R.U.B.E. is the acronym for Real Useful Box2D Editor (https://www.iforce2d.net/rube/). This editor allows you to graphically manipulate a Box2D world and import the physical objects into the game with no effort. The main advantage of having such a tool is that you will avoid the problem of writing the code of the physical elements of your game. As a consequence, you can focus in more important aspects, such as the logic of the game, instead of expending effort on editing the scene.

LevelHelper Pro

LevelHelper Pro is a tool that allows you to edit the scene for your game using the asset prepared with SpriteHelper Pro (http://www.gamedevhelper.com/levelhelper/). With this tool you can configure animations, create custom shapes, configure path movements, create the physic elements of a Box2D world, add parallaxes illusion, and many more.

Tiled

Tiled is flexible map editor (http://www.mapeditor.org/) that allows you to graphically create a scene using tiles.

Animation

Spine

Spine is a tool that allows you to create 2D skeletal animations for integration into your games (http://esotericsoftware.com/). The advantage of using skeletal animation in your game is that the amount of animations and memory consumption can be reduced substantially. Also, the animation looks smoother compare with an animation of a collection of sprites.

Utilities

Particle Designer

Particle Designer is a tool developed by 71Squared that allows you to create particle effects (http://71squared.com/en/particledesigner). This tool provides a gives you a dashboard of sliders and a preview so you can modify your particle system on the fly.

Glyph Designer

Glyph Designer is a tool developed by 71Squared that allows you to create bitmap fonts (http://71squared.com/en/glyphdesigner). With this tool bitmapped fonts atlas, which is a single texture file that contains all the characters together with a configuration file that indicates the location of each element.

SneakyJoystick Library

SneakyJoystick is a library created CJ Hanson (https://github.com/cjhanson) that allows you to include a joystick in your games. The library support:

* Joystick Thumb
* Joystick D-Pad
* Regular Buttons
* Holdable Buttons
* Toggleable Button

This library is used through the book to support and facilitate several examples presented here. You can find a port for Coco2d-x 3.0 at https://github.com/DragonBackGames/SneakyJoystick

CocoStudio

CocoStudio is a complete game development environment created for Cocos2d-x. This tool runs in both Windows and Mac OSX.

UI Editor

The UI Editor is a tool that allows you to create user interface objects for your game. Currently, there are 12 different kinds of user interface elements available in the tool.

Animator Editor

The Animator Editor is a tool that allows you to incorporate skeletal animation into your game. This is one alternative to the Spine tool.

Data Cruncher

The Data Cruncher is a tool that allows you to import data from Excel tables. This is used as a support for the Scene Editor.

Scene Editor

The Scene Editor is used to create scene for your game. You can incorporate the assets created with the UI Editor, Animator Editor and Data Cruncher into the scene. Additionally, you can incorporate assets created with third party tools.

Mobile App Monetization

In App Products is an API that allows you to create a virtual store inside your application. This API is referred as 'In App Purchase' on Apple development platform and as 'In App Billing' on Google development platform. The concept behind this feature consists in offering to the user the possibility of buying extra elements for your game such as new levels, extra lives, special items, etc.

The process behind buying an *in app product* is quite simple. When the user requests to buy an extra element; the application uses the framework to connect to the Apple Store or Google Play servers to perform a secure process payment. Once the payment is authorized the framework notifies the application, which provides the purchased items to the user.

Including monetization within your application depends highly on the target platform. However, there is a framework called SOOMLA (http://soom.la/), which provides the required features to include In App Purchases in your application more easily.

Summary

This chapter presented a complete list of supporting tools that could be used to power the development of your application. Some tools are open source and other requires paying a license. I would recommend you to give a try to each of the tools and select the one that best fit to your needs.

Sprites and Effects

This chapter provides the basis about sprites in Cocos2d-x. It explains the methods used to load the textures using images files and sprite sheets. There is also a description about the actions that can be associated to the sprites, and how to create animation using a sequence of images.

Go ahead and download the chapter files from https://github.com/DragonBackGames/BookCocos2DX/tree/master/CHAPTER_4. This folder contains a basic project with a template to work along this chapter.

Working with Sprites

Sprites are the images showed in the game scenes, which represent game elements such as the player, enemies, obstacles, background or anything that needs to be displayed. A sprite can be animated, moved or programmed to interact with other elements or with the user. Cocos2d-x supports several image file formats such as PNG, JPG or TIFF. In Cocos2d-x, sprites images are converted into textures and stored in a class called **Sprite**.

The two most common methods to load a sprite in Cocos2d-x are the following,

```
Sprite* m_image = Sprite::create("imageName.png");
Sprite* m_image = Sprite::createWithSpriteFrameName
      ("imageName.png");
```

To understand the different between both methods, you first need to know the concept of sprite sheet. A sprite sheet is a collection of sprites in a single image file. The main advantage of using sprite sheets is that multiple images are loaded at once reducing significantly the time to render the textures in your game. This is how a sprite sheet looks like.

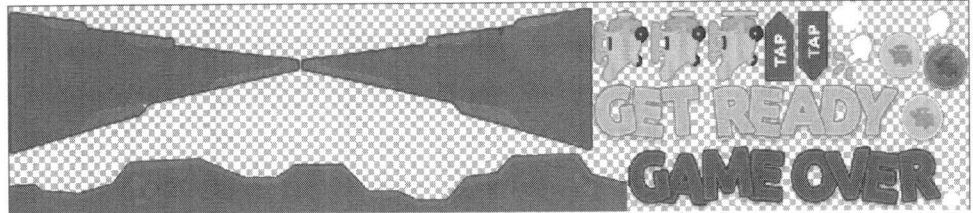

Let's write some code to understand how to use both methods. Open the file GameScene.cpp and at the init() method add the following code,

```cpp
bool GameScene::init()
{
    if (!Layer::init())
    {
        return false;
    }

    Size visibleSize = Director::getInstance()
            ->getVisibleSize();
    Point origin = Director::getInstance()
            ->getVisibleOrigin();

    auto bg = Sprite::create("GameBackground.png");
    bg->setPosition(Point(visibleSize.width/2
        + origin.x, visibleSize.height/2 + origin.y));
    this->addChild(bg,-1);

    SpriteFrameCache::getInstance()->addSpriteFramesWithFile
        ("GameSprites.plist","GameSprites.png");
    playerSprite = Sprite::createWithSpriteFrameName
        ("planeBlue1.png");
    playerSprite ->setPosition(Point(visibleSize.width * 0.2
        + origin.x, visibleSize.height/2 + origin.y));
    this->addChild(playerSprite);

    return true;
}
```

1. We create a sprite using `Sprite::create` for the background and set its position at the center of the screen.
2. We use the `SpriteFrameCache` to load the sprite sheet. The information relative to the position of each sprite within the sprite sheet is located in the .plist file.
3. We create a second sprite using `Sprite::createWithSpriteFrameName`.
4. Both sprites are added to the `Layer` to using `addChild` method.

Build and run the project, and you should see something like this.

Including Actions

Cocos2d-x offers the possibility to include actions on top of a sprite. There are lots of different kinds of actions that can be incorporated. For example, you can make a sprite to move, rotate, scale, jump, follow a certain path, blink, fade in, fade out, and many more. The **Test Project** provides an overview of all different alternatives provided by the engine. In Cocos2d-x actions are stored in a class called **Action**.

It's time to include some actions to the sprites included in the game. Put the following code right after the player sprite instantiation

```
auto windowSize = Director::getInstance()->getWinSize();
auto    movePlayerUp    =    MoveBy::create(1,    Point(0    ,
windowSize.height * 0.2));
auto movePlayerDown = movePlayerUp->reverse();
auto delay = DelayTime::create(0.25f);
auto sequencePlayer = Sequence::create(movePlayerUp,
        delay, movePlayerDown, delay->clone(), NULL);
playerSprite-
>runAction(RepeatForever::create(sequencePlayer));
```

1. We create a move action using `MoveBy::create` to change the position of the sprite, and set the action duration and destination point
2. We create a second move action which is a reverse from the first action
3. With `Sequence::create` we specify the sequence of actions that are executed on top of the object
4. We tell to the `playerSprite` to run an action that contains the previous sequence forever

Let's add another action to the plane.

```
// Create a cardinal action
auto trajectoryArray = PointArray::create(9);
trajectoryArray->addControlPoint(Point(visibleSize.width
* 0.9  + origin.x, visibleSize.height * 0.6 + origin.y));
trajectoryArray->addControlPoint(Point(visibleSize.width
* 0.8 + origin.x, visibleSize.height * 0.7 + origin.y));
trajectoryArray->addControlPoint(Point(visibleSize.width
* 0.7 + origin.x, visibleSize.height * 0.6 + origin.y));
trajectoryArray->addControlPoint(Point(visibleSize.width
* 0.6 + origin.x, visibleSize.height * 0.5 + origin.y));
trajectoryArray->addControlPoint(Point(visibleSize.width
* 0.5 + origin.x, visibleSize.height * 0.6 + origin.y));
trajectoryArray->addControlPoint(Point(visibleSize.width
* 0.6 + origin.x, visibleSize.height * 0.7 + origin.y));
```

```
trajectoryArray->addControlPoint(Point(visibleSize.width
* 0.7 + origin.x, visibleSize.height * 0.6 + origin.y));
trajectoryArray->addControlPoint(Point(visibleSize.width
* 0.8 + origin.x, visibleSize.height * 0.5 + origin.y));
trajectoryArray->addControlPoint(Point(visibleSize.width
* 0.9 + origin.x, visibleSize.height * 0.6 + origin.y));

auto cardinalAction = CardinalSplineBy::create
      (3, trajectoryArray, 0);
playerSprite ->runAction(cardinalAction);
```

1. We create an array that contains a trajectory of points. The idea is that the object moves across this trajectory
2. We create a Cardinal Spline action using `CardinalSplineBy::create` by specifying the duration of the action, the trajectory points and the tension
3. We tell to the sprite to run the action that we created

Build and run the project, and you should see sprites moving across the screen.

Using Animations

In Cocos2d-x, an animation consists in an action that changes the current texture of a sprite across the time. To create an animation, you need to store the sequence of texture in an object of type **Animation** and then associate to an action **Animate** the object previously created.

Let's create a simple animation in order to understand better the concept. Open the file `GameScene.cpp` and add the following code just right after where you left on the previous section,

```
// Plane animation
auto planeAnimation = Animation::create();
for(int index = 1; index < 4; index++ )
{
    char name[50] = {0};
    sprintf(name, "planeBlue%i.png", index);
```

```cpp
    SpriteFrame* planeSpriteFrame =
            SpriteFrameCache::getInstance()->
                getSpriteFrameByName(name);
    planeAnimation->addSpriteFrame(planeSpriteFrame);
}

planeAnimation->setDelayPerUnit(0.3f / 3.0f);
planeAnimation->setRestoreOriginalFrame(true);
auto planeAnimate = Animate::create(planeAnimation);
auto planeRepeatForever =
    RepeatForever::create(planeAnimate);
playerSprite->runAction(planeRepeatForever);

// Puff animation
auto puffAnimation = Animation::create();
char name[50] = {0};
SpriteFrame* puffSpriteFrame;
sprintf(name, "puffLarge.png");
puffSpriteFrame = SpriteFrameCache::getInstance()->
            getSpriteFrameByName(name);
puffAnimation->addSpriteFrame(puffSpriteFrame);
sprintf(name, "puffSmall.png");
puffSpriteFrame = SpriteFrameCache::getInstance()->
            getSpriteFrameByName(name);
puffAnimation->addSpriteFrame(puffSpriteFrame);

puffAnimation->setDelayPerUnit(0.2f / 2.0f);
puffAnimation->setRestoreOriginalFrame(true);
auto puffAnimate = Animate::create(puffAnimation);
auto puffRepeatForever =
            RepeatForever::create(puffAnimate);
auto puffSprite = Sprite::create();
puffSprite->runAction(puffRepeatForever);
puffSprite->setPosition(Point
        (-playerSprite->getContentSize().width * 0.3,
        playerSprite->getContentSize().height * 0.7));
playerSprite->addChild(puffSprite);
```

1. We create an animation using `Animation::create` for the plane animation
2. We create and add the frames to the animation by loading the textures using `SpriteFrameCache::getInstance()` `->getSpriteFrameByName`
3. We configure the delay of the animation and we set that the animation goes back to the first frame once the animation sequence is completed
4. We create an **Animate** action using the previous animation and we create a **Repeat Forever** action in order to see the same sequence forever
5. We assign the action to the player sprite
6. We repeat the same process to create an animation of the puff
7. We create a sprite for the puff and we associate the action that we just configured before.
8. We add the puff sprite to the player sprite. By doing this the puff will move together with the player.

Build and run the project, and you should see how the plane and puff are animated.

Summary

Throughout this chapter you learned how to manipulate sprites on Cocos2d-x. These are the basis to build any of your games. You also learned the basis of actions and animations. Try to take advantage of the actions provided by the engine. These features will definitely be a time saver at the time you will be developing your application. In the following chapter more interesting features will be added to the game.

Multiple Layers and Multiple Scenes

This chapter explains the basis about layers and scenes. It explains how to use multiple layers and multiple scenes within your game. It also describes how to use the Director to switch between the different scenes.

Go ahead and download the chapter files from https://github.com/DragonBackGames/BookCocos2DX/tree/master/CHAPTER_5. This folder contains a basic project with a template to work along this chapter.

Game Architecture in Cocos2d-x

In Cocos2d-x, the main elements of the game architecture consist in scenes, layers and nodes. A scene is an independent part of the application. It can be interpreted as a stage or screen in your game.

To control which scene is active in the game, Cocos2d-x provides the class Director. The Director is a single object that selects which is the current scene to show in the game. At Cocos2d-x, the Director can handle only one scene at the time.

A scene contains one or more layers. The layers are used as containers to store nodes, such as sprites, menus, labels, and others. Layers can handle events, which are used to modify the state of your game.

Working with Multiple Layers

In Cocos2d-x, layers are stored in the class **Layer**. Layers are semi-transparent, allowing the user to superimpose other layers without hiding the content. Typically, a scene contains multiple layers; which are used to define different sections of the screen such as the background, animation, controls, scores, menus and many others.

Open the project relative to this chapter. You will notice that the template separates the files in directories. This is just to give a better organization for the project. The directory **Layers** includes the files relative to the layers for the game.

Open the **ControllerLayer.h** file and add the following code,

```
class ControllerLayer : public Layer
{
    // Destructor
    ~ControlGameLayer();
    // Create a layer
    static ControlGameLayer* create();
    // Returns state of buttons
    CC_SYNTHESIZE_READONLY(Point, stickPosition,
            StickPosition);
    CC_SYNTHESIZE_READONLY(bool, attackButtonValue,
            AttackButtonValue);

private:
    // standard Cocos2d layer method
    virtual bool init();
    // standard Cocos2d layer method
    virtual void update(float dt);
    // Click play button callback
    void clickPauseButton(Ref* sender);

    // Joystick
    SneakyJoystick* leftJoystick;
    // Attack button
    SneakyButton *attackButton;
    // Pause menu item
    MenuItemSprite* pauseMenuItem;
};
```

1. We defined a static method called `create()` which returns a `ControllerLayer` object
2. We use **SneakyJoystick** library to include one joystick thumb and the attack button to the layer
3. We add a menu for the pause button
4. We provide helper methods to retrieve the value of such elements

Open the **ControllerLayer.cpp** file and add the following code to the `create()` method,

```
ControllerLayer* ControllerLayer::create()
{
    ControllerLayer* layer = new ControlGameLayer();
    layer->init();
    return layer;
}
```

Now, under the same file add the following code to the `init()` method,

```
bool ControlGameLayer::init()
{
    if (!Layer::init())
    {
    return false;
    }

    Size screenSize = Director::getInstance()
        ->getWinSize();

    SpriteFrameCache::getInstance()->
      addSpriteFramesWithFile("ControllerSceneSprite.plist",
      "ControllerSceneSprite.png");

    // Configure joystick
    Point joystickBasePosition;
    joystickBasePosition = Point(screenSize.width * 0.2f,
        screenSize.height*0.2f);
```

```
SneakyJoystickSkinnedBase *joystickBase = new
        SneakyJoystickSkinnedBase();
joystickBase->init();
joystickBase->setPosition(joystickBasePosition);
joystickBase->setBackgroundSprite
        (Sprite::createWithSpriteFrameName
                ("backgroundJoy.png"));
joystickBase->setThumbSprite
        (Sprite::createWithSpriteFrameName
                ("thumbJoy.png"));

Rect joystickBaseDimensions;
joystickBaseDimensions = CCRectMake(0, 0, 160.0f,
        160.0f);
SneakyJoystick *aJoystick = new SneakyJoystick();
aJoystick->initWithRect(joystickBaseDimensions);
aJoystick->autorelease();
joystickBase->setJoystick(aJoystick);
joystickBase->setPosition(joystickBasePosition);

leftJoystick = joystickBase->getJoystick();
leftJoystick->retain();
this->addChild(joystickBase);
...
```

1. We start by configuring the joystick thumb, by creating a `SneakyJoystickSkinnedBase` object. This object stores the textures for the joystick
2. We create a `SneakyJoystick` object with a predefine dimension. This object is attached to the Skinned Base that we created before
3. Finally, we assign to the data member `leftJoystick` the joystick associated to the Skinned Base and we retain it to avoid losing its reference

We continue with the configuration of the layer by adding the attack button,

```
...
//Create Attack Button
```

```
Point attackButtonPosition;
attackButtonPosition = Point
    (screenSize.width * 0.85f, screenSize.height
        * 0.2f);

SneakyButtonSkinnedBase *attackButtonBase =
    new SneakyButtonSkinnedBase();
attackButtonBase->init();
attackButtonBase->setPosition(attackButtonPosition);

attackButtonBase->setDefaultSprite
    (Sprite::createWithSpriteFrameName
        ("attackBtn.png"));
attackButtonBase->setActivatedSprite
    (Sprite::createWithSpriteFrameName
        ("attackBtn.png"));
attackButtonBase->setDisabledSprite
    (Sprite::createWithSpriteFrameName
        ("attackBtn.png"));
attackButtonBase->setPressSprite
    (Sprite::createWithSpriteFrameName
        ("attackBtn.png"));
Rect attackButtonDimensions = CCRectMake
    (0, 0, 96.0f, 96.0f);
SneakyButton *aAttackButton = new SneakyButton();
aAttackButton->initWithRect(attackButtonDimensions);
aAttackButton->autorelease();

attackButtonBase->setButton(aAttackButton);
attackButtonBase->setPosition(attackButtonPosition);

attackButton = attackButtonBase->getButton();
attackButton->retain();
this->addChild(attackButtonBase);
...
```

1. We follow the same procedure to create the buttons. We start the configuration by creating a `SneakyButtonSkinnedBase` object. For the

buttons you can define a texture for four different states of the button, **Default, Activated, Disabled** and **Press**.

2. We create a `SneakyButton` object with a predefine dimension. This object is attached to the Skinned Base that we created before
3. Finally, we assign to the data member `attackJoystick` the joystick associated to the Skinned Base and we retain it to avoid losing its reference

We continue by adding the pause menu

```
    auto pauseOn =
Sprite::createWithSpriteFrameName("pauseBtn.png");
    auto pauseOff =
Sprite::createWithSpriteFrameName("pauseBtn.png");
    pauseMenuItem = MenuItemSprite::create(pauseOn, pauseOff,

        CC_CALLBACK_1(ControlGameLayer::clickPauseButton,
        this));

    auto pauseMenu = Menu::create(pauseMenuItem, NULL);
    pauseMenu->setPosition(Point(screenSize.width * 0.9f,
            screenSize.height * 0.9f));
    this->addChild(pauseMenu, 1);
    ...
```

1. We add the textures for the pause button on default and on press state
2. We create a `MenuItemSprite` in which we indicate the menu texture and the callback to run when the button is pressed
3. We create a menu and added to the layer

Finally, we add `scheduleUpdate()` and `setTouchEnabled(true)` to enable a game loop task and the reception of touches by the layer.

Now that we have our controller layer ready, we can proceed to add it to the scene. Open the file `GameScene.cpp` and add the following code at the `initControllers()` method

```
ControlGameLayer* GameScene::initControllers()
```

```
{
    this->controlGameLayer = ControlGameLayer::create();
    return this->controlGameLayer;
}
```

and to the `createScene()` method

```
Scene* GameScene::createScene()
{
    // 'scene' is an autorelease object
    auto scene = Scene::create();

    // 'layer' is an autorelease object
    auto layer = GameScene::create();

    // add layer as a child to scene
    scene->addChild(layer);

    // Add controller layer
    scene->addChild(layer->initControllers(), 1);
    ...
```

1. We create an instance of the `ControlGameLayer` object
2. We add the control game layer instance as child to the scene

If you build and run the project, you should see something like this

Workings with Multiple Scenes

In Cocos2d-x, scenes are stored in the class **Scene**. As described before scenes represent the different screens of your game. Let's continue with the example relative to this chapter to include the different scenes of the game. Inside the directory **Scenes**, there are three scenes **Menu Scene**, **Settings Scene** and **Game Scene**.

First, let's modify the scene that is called by default. Open the `AppDelegate.cpp` file and change the line

```
auto scene = GameScene::createScene();
```

for

```
auto scene = MenuScene::createScene();
```

Add also on top of the file `#include "MenuScene.h"`.

Open the `MenuScene.cpp` file, and add the following code at the `initControllers` method.

```
Size screenSize = Director::getInstance()->getWinSize();

    // Create pause menu
    auto playOn =
Sprite::createWithSpriteFrameName("playOnBtn.png");
    auto playOff =
Sprite::createWithSpriteFrameName("playOffBtn.png");
    playMenuItem = MenuItemSprite::create(playOn, playOff,
CC_CALLBACK_1(MenuScene::clickPlayButton, this));

    auto settingsOn =
Sprite::createWithSpriteFrameName("settingsOnBtn.png");
    auto settingsOff =
Sprite::createWithSpriteFrameName("settingsOffBtn.png");
    settingsMenuItem = MenuItemSprite::create(settingsOn,
settingsOff, CC_CALLBACK_1(MenuScene::clickSettingsButton,
this));

    auto mainMenu = Menu::create(playMenuItem,
settingsMenuItem, NULL);
    mainMenu->setPosition(Point(screenSize.width * 0.7f,
screenSize.height * 0.4f));
    mainMenu->alignItemsVerticallyWithPadding(20);
    this->addChild(mainMenu, 1);
```

1. We create a two `MenuItemSprite` objects that represents the two
   buttons of the menu: one for the **Play** button and one for the **Settings**
   button. At the configuration we select which image is shown when the button
   is pressed or not. Also, we specify which method is called when the button is
   pressed.
2. We create a Menu specifying the different menu items. We align them
   vertically and set up its position.
3. Finally, we add the menu as a child to the layer

Let's continue under the same file and edit the method `clickPlayButton`

```
Scene* newScene = TransitionMoveInR::create(0.2f,
GameScene::createScene());
Director::getInstance()->replaceScene(newScene);
```

1. We create a **Transition Move** to load an instance of **GameScene**
2. We tell to the Director to replace the current scene with the previous one create

Finally, we edit the `clickSettingsButton` method,

```
Scene* newScene = TransitionMoveInR::create(0.2f,
SettingsScene::scene());
Director::getInstance()->replaceScene(newScene);
```

Open the `SettingsScene.cpp` file, and add the following code at the `initControllers` method.

```
    Size screenSize = Director::getInstance()->getWinSize();

    // Create back menu
    auto backOn =
Sprite::createWithSpriteFrameName("backOnBtn.png");
    auto backOff =
Sprite::createWithSpriteFrameName("backOffBtn.png");
    backMenuItem = MenuItemSprite::create(backOn, backOff,
            CC_CALLBACK_1(SettingsScene::clickBackButton,
      this));

    auto backMenu = Menu::create(backMenuItem, NULL);
    backMenu->setPosition(Point(screenSize.width * 0.1f,
            screenSize.height * 0.9f));
    this->addChild(backMenu, 1);
```

1. Similar to the previous, we create a menu item, which contains the back button. The callback function relative to the press button event is specified here
2. We add the menu as a child to the layer

Let's continue under the same file and edit the method `clickBackButton`

```
Scene* newScene = TransitionMoveInR::create(0.2f,
MenuScene::createScene());
Director::getInstance()->replaceScene(newScene);
```

Open the `ControlGameLayer.cpp` file, and add the following code at the `clickPauseButton` method,

```
Scene* newScene = TransitionMoveInR::create
        (0.2f, MenuScene::createScene());
Director::getInstance()->replaceScene(newScene);
```

For the sake of simplicity, we will use the pause button to go back to the main menu. This will change later as the game evolves throughout the book.

If you build and run the application, you will notice how the scenes change as you press the buttons.

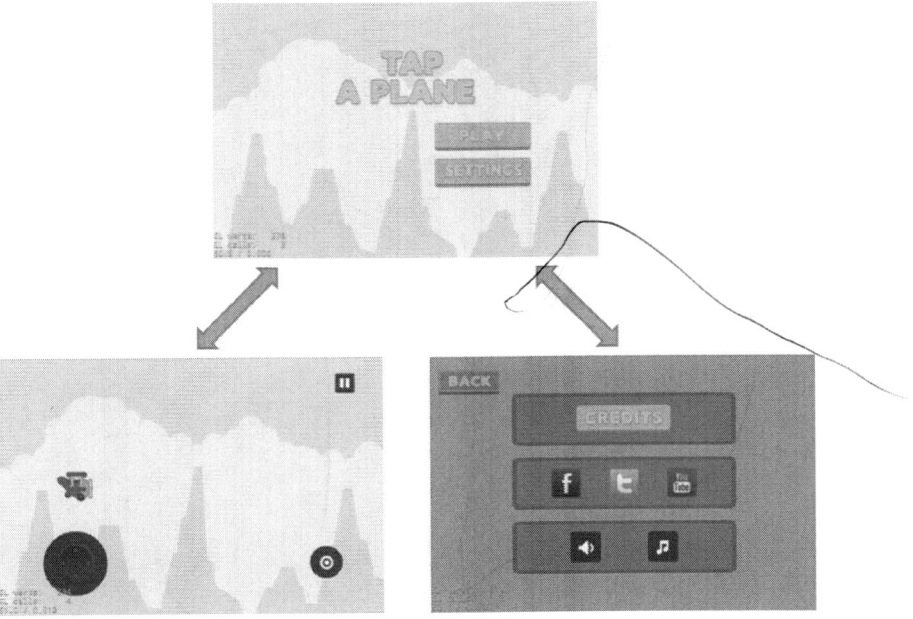

Summary

In this chapter you learned how to manipulate multiple layers and scenes with Cocos2d-x. This will allow you to structure correctly the content of your game. Another trick that you could include on your scenes is to create them as Singletons. Following this approach, the application won't need to load the textures each time that you switch from one scene to another.

Game Loop and Events

This chapter provides additional elements related with the configuration and control of the game logic. It describes how to configure the game loop and how to include touches events

Go ahead and download the chapter files from https://github.com/DragonBackGames/BookCocos2DX/tree/master/CHAPTER_6. This folder contains a basic project with a template to work along this chapter.

Game Scheduler

Like any other software application, a game can be described as a state machine. Depending on the next event, the game will execute a certain action. For example, if the player kills an enemy the state machine will trigger an animation showing how the enemy dies, then the enemy object should be removed from the layer and finally the score should be incremented depending on which kind of enemy was killed.

The state machine should run periodically in order to verify which action to execute next depending on the events that arrive. For this purpose, Cocos2d-x provides two different types of callbacks,

- Update selector: a method called update can be invoked every frame with the possibility of configuring the priority
- Custom selector: a custom method can be invoked every frame or within a custom interval

You can ensure the invocation of the `update` method by using `scheduleUpdate()`.

Let's write some code to understand how to scheduler works. Open the file ControlGameLayer.cpp and at the end of the init() method add scheduleUpdate().

Continue by adding the following code on for the update method

```cpp
void ControlGameLayer::update(float dt)
{
    stickPosition = leftJoystick->getStickPosition();
    attackButtonValue = attackButton->getIsActive();
}
```

1. We retrieve the joystick position to store it in a variable that can be accessible by the Game Scene
2. We perform the same for the attack button to know when the button is pressed

Now, open the file GameScene.cpp and at the end of the init() method add also scheduleUpdate().

Continue by adding the following code on for the update method

```cpp
Point stickPosition = controlGameLayer->getStickPosition();
bool attackButtonValue =
    controlGameLayer->getAttackButtonValue();

auto movePlayer = MoveBy::create(dt,
    Point(stickPosition.x / 10.0, stickPosition.y / 10.0));
playerSprite->runAction(movePlayer);
```

1. We retrieve the position of the joystick and the attack button value from the controller layer
2. We move the plane according to the position of the joystick using a Move action

If you build and run the application, you will notice how the plane moves together with the joystick.

Touch Events

Another alternative to control the player in the game is through touch events. In the case of our game, we will use touch events to allow the player jump across the screen. Cocos2d-x allows you to handle four types of touch events, Touch Began, Touch Moved, Touch Ended and Touch Cancelled.

Since the Cocos2d-x 3.0 the touch events, keyboard events, acceleration events and custom events are dispatched by the EventDispatcher class. The method setTouchEnabled is deprecated since the latest version.

To exemplify the usage of these events open the open the file GameScene.cpp and add the following code at the end of the init() method

```
auto listener = EventListenerTouchOneByOne::create();
listener->setSwallowTouches(true);
listener->onTouchBegan =
     CC_CALLBACK_2(GameScene::onTouchBegan, this);
listener->onTouchMoved =
     CC_CALLBACK_2(GameScene::onTouchMoved, this);
listener->onTouchEnded =
     CC_CALLBACK_2(GameScene::onTouchEnded, this);
listener->onTouchCancelled =
     CC_CALLBACK_2(GameScene::onTouchCancelled, this);
_eventDispatcher->
     addEventListenerWithSceneGraphPriority(listener, this);
```

1. We create a Touch Event listener object
2. We assign the touch event callbacks to the GameScene touch methods
3. We add to the EventDispatcher the created listener.

Under the same file, let's edit the onTouchBegan method by adding the following code

```
auto jumpPlayerUp = JumpBy::create(1, Point(80, 0), 100, 1);
auto seqPlayerUp = Sequence::create(jumpPlayerUp, NULL);
playerSprite->runAction(seqPlayerUp);
return true;
```

1. We create a move action using `JumpBy::create` to make the sprite jump on the screen
2. With `Sequence::create` we specify the sequence of actions that are executed on top of the object
3. We tell to the `playerSprite` to run an action that contains the previous sequence

If you build and run the application, you will notice how the plane jumps when the screen is touched.

Summary

In this chapter you learned how to use the game scheduler. This allows you to include a state machine into your application. You saw how to use the joystick to move the player across the screen and also how to handle the touch events.

Physics Engines

In Cocos2d-x it is possible to integrate one of the two most popular 2D physic engines: Box2D and Chipmunk. This chapter focuses only on the integration and usage of Box2D within Cocos2d-x.

Go ahead and download the chapter files from https://github.com/DragonBackGames/BookCocos2DX/tree/master/CHAPTER_7. This folder contains a basic project with a template to work along this chapter.

Introduction to Box2D

A physic engine is a software component that provides a simulation of a certain physical system, as for example rigid body dynamics, soft body dynamics and fluid dynamics. Box2D is an open source physic engine that simulates rigid body dynamics in 2D. It provides several features such as collision detection, contact callback, multiple shapes for rigid bodies, several types joint types, different kinds of physic behaviour such as contact, friction, and momentum just to name a few. Generally speaking, including a physic engine provides you with countless features that enrich your games.

Configuring Box2D on Cocos2d-x 3.0

Box2D is already contained as default in the new projects that you create with Cocos2d-x tools. However, if you are using Microsoft Visual Studio an additional procedure is required to configure properly the library.

1. Right click on **Solutions** and select **Add->Existing Projects**. Inside your project directory navigate into **cocos2d\external\Box2D\proj.win32** and add the **Box2D.vcxproj** project

2. Right click again on **Solutions** and select **Properties**. On the **Project Dependencies** select your project from the combo box. On the **Depends on** list check **libBox2D**
3. Right click on your game project and select **Properties**. Under **Common Properties->Framework and References** click on the button **Add New Reference**. Check on the **libBox2D** and click **OK**
4. To verify that Box2D was properly configured, right click again on your game project and select **Properties**. Under **Configuration Properties->Linker-> Command Line** you will see a list with all the options. Check that **libBox2D.lib** is in that list.

Getting Started with Box2D

Box2D could be summarized in four kinds of objects: worlds, bodies, fixtures and joints.

Worlds define the main entity where all the physic elements live. You use a world to create or destroy bodies, define gravity, tune physics simulation, find a fixture, etc. To understand how to use this object, open the `GameScene.cpp` file and include the following code on the `initPhysics` method,

```
b2Vec2 gravity;
gravity.Set(0.0f, -10.0f);
world = new b2World(gravity);
```

1. We configure the gravity of the world equal to -10. You can also configure the gravity dynamically if it is needed
2. We create a new world object

Once you create a world, you need to allow the simulation to take place. Now, under the `update` method include the following code,

```
float32 timeStep = dt;
int32 velocityIterations = 8;
int32 positionIterations = 3;
```

```
world->Step( timeStep, velocityIterations,
        positionIterations);
```

1. We configure the length of the time passed to simulate equal to the update delta time.
2. We configure the correction of the velocity to 8.
3. We configure the correction of the position to 3.
4. We tell to the world to perform a step on the simulation

Bodies are the fundamentals objects of the of the physic environment. The bodies define properties such as mass, velocity, rotational inertia, angular velocity, location and angle. The size and shape are defined by the fixtures. Box2D provides three different kinds of bodies,

- Static bodies, a body that does not move under simulation and behaves as it has infinite mass. Static bodies can be moved manually, their velocity is zero, and they do not collide with other static bodies or kinematic bodies
- Dynamic bodies, a body that is fully simulated. Dynamic bodies respond to forces, they can collide with all body types. Their mass is finite
- Kinematic bodies, a body that moves under simulation according to its velocity. Kinematic bodies do not respond to forces. They can be moved by setting its velocity. Their mass is infinite and they do not collide with static or kinematic bodies

Now continue on the GameScene.cpp file, and include the following code at the method initPhysics,

```
b2BodyDef myBodyDef;
myBodyDef.type = b2_dynamicBody;
myBodyDef.position.Set(0, 20);
myBodyDef.angle = 0;
b2Body* dynamicBody = m_world->CreateBody(&myBodyDef);
```

1. We define the properties of the body, by specifying the type as dynamic, the initial position and angle

2. We create a body using the object world

Fixtures are used to define the size and shape of the body. A body can have multiple fixtures associated to it. The main properties of a fixture are shape, restitution, friction and density. You can create different shapes such as rectangles, circles or polygons. Let's continue were we just left and add the following code,

```
b2PolygonShape boxShape;
boxShape.SetAsBox(1,1);
b2FixtureDef boxFixtureDef;
boxFixtureDef.shape = &boxShape;
boxFixtureDef.density = 1;
dynamicBody->CreateFixture(&boxFixtureDef);
```

1. We create a polygon shape and define the shape as a box
2. We define a fixture and define the shape as the polygon created before
3. We create a fixture with the dynamic body previously created using the method `CreateFixture`

Joints are used to connect two bodies together. They can be used to simulate interaction between objects such as hinges, pistons, ropes, pulleys, etc. The joints offered by Box2D are,

- Revolute, a hinge or pin, where the bodies rotate about a common point
- Distance, a point on each body will be kept at a fixed distance apart
- Prismatic, the relative rotation of the two bodies is fixed, and they can slide along an axis
- Line, a combination of revolute and prismatic joints
- Weld, holds the bodies at the same orientation
- Pulley, a point on each body will be kept within a certain distance from a point in the world
- Friction, reduces the relative motion between the two bodies
- Gear, controls two other joints (revolute or prismatic) so that the movement of one affects the other

- Mouse, pulls a point on one body to a location in the world

Box2D by itself does not give directly a mean to visualize the shapes on the screen. Instead, the engine provides an extension to connect a library for rendering the objects using OpenGL ES. Here we will explain how to use GLES-Render library for debugging purposes.

Under the GameScene.cpp file under the initPhysics method add the following code,

```
debugDraw = new GLESDebugDraw( PTM_RATIO );
debugDraw->SetFlags
       ( b2Draw::e_shapeBit | b2Draw::e_jointBit );
world->SetDebugDraw(debugDraw);
```

1. We create an instance of the GLESDebugDraw debug class. We pass as an argument the pixel to meter ratio. Typically, this value is equal to 32
2. We configure the debugger to renderer the shapes and joints
3. We assign to the world the debug object

Continue ahead and edit the draw method with the following code

```
void GameScene::draw(Renderer *renderer,
       const kmMat4 &transform, bool transformUpdated)
{
    // Standard Cocos2d method
    if (!world)
    {
        return;
    }

    // debug draw display will be on top of anything else
    Layer::draw(renderer, transform, transformUpdated);

    ccGLEnableVertexAttribs( kCCVertexAttribFlag_Position );
    kmGLPushMatrix();
    world->DrawDebugData();
    kmGLPopMatrix();
}
```

The previous code calls the debugger to render the shapes on the screen.

If you build and run the application, you should see the bodies draw using OpenGL ES.

Decorating Bodies with Sprites

Associating a body with sprites it is an important subject to consider while using a physic engine in your game. Box2D offer the possibility to address this topic by including the property userData within the body objects.

The user data can consists in a class or a structure that contains all extra attributes to be carried out by the body object. In our case, we create a structure called ObstacleUserData.

```
enum FixtureType
{
      FT_PLAYER,
      FT_PICKUP,
      FT_ROCK
};

struct ObstacleUserData
{
      FixtureType fixtureType;
      b2Body* body;
      CCSprite* sprite;
};
```

Instead of hardcoding the fixtures for the bodies, one alternative is to use a tool that creates the shape for you. The tool that I used for this example is **PhysicsEditor**, which is described at the chapter **Toolset and Support**.

Once you create the object file, add the following code at the end of initPhysics,

```
GB2ShapeCache::sharedGB2ShapeCache()->
```

```
        addShapesWithFile("GameSceneObjects.plist");

auto screenSize = Director::getInstance()->getWinSize();

b2BodyDef myBodyDef;
myBodyDef.type = b2_dynamicBody;
myBodyDef.position.Set(screenSize.width * 0.2 / PTM_RATIO,
        screenSize.height * 0.5 / PTM_RATIO);
myBodyDef.angle = 0;
playerBody = world->CreateBody(&myBodyDef);


ObstacleUserData* playerUserData = new ObstacleUserData;
playerUserData->body = playerBody;
playerUserData->sprite = playerSprite;
playerUserData->fixtureType = FT_PLAYER;
playerBody->SetUserData((void*)playerUserData);

GB2ShapeCache::sharedGB2ShapeCache()->
        addFixturesToBody(playerBody, "planeRed1");
playerSprite>
        setAnchorPoint(GB2ShapeCache::sharedGB2ShapeCache()->
        anchorPointForShape("planeRed1"));

for (b2Fixture* f = playerBody->GetFixtureList(); f;
        f = f->GetNext())
{
    playerFixture = f;
}
```

1. We create a dynamic body and assign its position
2. Configure the user data by setting the body, sprite and type
3. Retrieve from the **Object File** the fixture of the object and assigned it to the player fixture.

As you can see creating a complex fixture for a body is quite straightforward with this tool. Once you assigned the user data to the body, add the following code at the update method to complete the decoration,

```
for (b2Body* b = world->GetBodyList(); b; b = b->GetNext())
{
        if (b->GetUserData() != NULL)
        {
        //Synchronize the AtlasSprites position
        //and rotation with the corresponding body
        ObstacleUserData * myActor = (ObstacleUserData *)
                b->GetUserData();
        myActor->sprite->setPosition
        ( CCPointMake( b->GetPosition().x * PTM_RATIO,
                b->GetPosition().y * PTM_RATIO) );
        myActor->sprite->setRotation
                ( -1 * CC_RADIANS_TO_DEGREES(b->GetAngle()) );
        }
}
```

1. We retrieve the user data from the body
2. We assign the position of the sprite equal to the body position scaled to the pixel to meter ratio
3. We assign the angle of the sprite to the body angle converted from radians to degrees

If you build and run the application, you should see the bodies draw using OpenGL ES and the sprites on top of it. If you want to remove the debug data just comment the code that you added at the `draw` method.

Moving Bodies

There are basically three ways of moving bodies setting velocity directly, using forces and using impulses.

You can set manually the velocity of the body by including the following code at the `onTouchBegan` method,

```
b2Vec2 playerVelocity = playerBody->GetLinearVelocity();
playerVelocity.y = 10;
playerBody->SetLinearVelocity(playerVelocity);
```

If you instead want to apply forces to the body, you can include the following code,

```
playerBody->ApplyForce( b2Vec2(0,2000), playerBody->
      GetWorldCenter(), true );
```

Finally, if you want to apply an impulse to the body, you should include the following code,

```
playerBody->ApplyImpulse( b2Vec2(0,70), playerBody->
      GetWorldCenter(), true );
```

Try the different options and select the one that is the most adequate for your situation depending on which behavior you want to simulate in your game.

Collision Detection

Box2D handles all the necessary collision detection between bodies during the simulation. To respond properly to the collision, you should specify to the word a callback that handles the action associated to the event.

First you must specify a Contact Listener object at the GameScene.h file,

```
class GameLayerContactListener : public b2ContactListener
{
public:
    // called by Box2D during the Step function
    // when two fixtures begin touching
      virtual void BeginContact(b2Contact* contact);
    // called by Box2D during the Step function
   // when two fixtures finish touching
     virtual void EndContact(b2Contact* contact);
     class GameScene* m_layer;
};
```

The `BeginContact` function in this class is called by Box2D during the `Step` function. We can use the info in the contact to see which two fixtures collided, but we cannot play with the Box2D world inside the contact listener because it gets grumpy if it is disturbed while busy.

Instead, this class holds a reference to the main layer, which it will use to update some variables to let the layer know something needs to be done after the physics `Step` has completed.

First we add the following code at the `initPhysics` method,

```
// Create contact listener
contactListener = new GameSceneContactListener();
world->SetContactListener(contactListener);
contactListener->m_layer = this;
```

Then, we implement the `BeginContact` function at the `GameScene.cpp` file,

```
void GameLayerContactListener::BeginContact
        (b2Contact* contact)
{
    GameScene* layer = (GameScene*)m_layer;
    b2Fixture* fA = contact->GetFixtureA();
    b2Fixture* fB = contact->GetFixtureB();

    if( fA == NULL || fB == NULL || layer == NULL)
    {
        return;
    }
    ObstacleUserData* fudA = (ObstacleUserData*)
            fA->GetBody()->GetUserData();
    ObstacleUserData* fudB = (ObstacleUserData*)
            fB->GetBody()->GetUserData();

    // Player hit a pick up
    if ( fudA && fudA->fixtureType == FT_PICKUP &&
```

```
            fB->GetBody() == layer->getPlayerBody() )
    {

    }
    if ( fudB && fudB->fixtureType == FT_PICKUP &&
            fA->GetBody() == layer->getPlayerBody() )
    {

    }

    // Player hit a rock
    if ( fudA && fudA->fixtureType == FT_ROCK &&
            fB->GetBody() == layer->getPlayerBody() )
    {

    }
    if ( fudB && fudB->fixtureType == FT_ROCK &&
            fA->GetBody() == layer->getPlayerBody() )
    {

    }
}

void GameSceneContactListener::
    EndContact(b2Contact* contact)
{

}
```

1. First we assign to the world the contact listener. We specify also the attributes of the contact listener
2. We define the `BeginContact` method by specifying if the object is colliding with a pick up or with a rock.
3. For the purpose of this game there are no actions defined at the `EndContact` method

At this moment the collisions does not have any impact on the game itself. This subject will remain open in the mean time and it will be completed later in the next chapter of the book.

Summary

In this chapter you learned how to use the Box2D together with Cocos2d-x. You saw the basis about the physic engine and how to debug the application using OpenGL renderer. You learned how to decorate a body with sprites, how to move the bodies and detect collision between them.

Game Layout

This chapter describes the how to create the game layout for your games. It presents how to create with an editor the content of the levels, how to scroll across the screen and how to add parallax effect.

Go ahead and download the chapter files from https://github.com/DragonBackGames/BookCocos2DX/tree/master/CHAPTER_8. This folder contains a basic project with a template to work along this chapter.

Building the Game Layout

While creating your game layout, you can chose between coding and using a support tool. The selection depends on the type of game that you are planning to do. As described in the chapter **Toolset and Support**, there are few tools available in the market that can be used for this purpose.

For our game we will use a combination of both. The layout consists in a group of rocks that are randomly located on the screen, and some pickups represented as stars that the plane takes to increase the score. The objects are Box2D bodies and the fixtures are created using the **PhysicsEditor** tool.

Let's start by adding the floor and ceiling for the layout. Open the `ObstacleLayer.cpp` and add the following code at the `generateObstacle` method.

```
auto screenSize = Director::getInstance()->getWinSize();
obstacleCounter += quantity;
// Update offset
int offsetEnd = offset + quantity;
// Generate floor and celing
for(; offset < offsetEnd; offset++)
{
        // Floor
```

```
b2BodyDef floorBodyDef;
floorBodyDef.position.Set(800 * offset / PTM_RATIO, 0);
b2Body* floorBody = world->CreateBody(&floorBodyDef);
GB2ShapeCache::sharedGB2ShapeCache()->
     addFixturesToBody(floorBody, "groundDirt");
Sprite* floorSprite =
Sprite::createWithSpriteFrameName("groundDirt.png");
floorSprite->setAnchorPoint(Point(0,0));
floorSprite->setPosition(Point(floorBody->
     GetPosition().x * PTM_RATIO, floorBody->
     GetPosition().y * PTM_RATIO));
this->addChild(floorSprite);

ObstacleUserData* floorUserData = new ObstacleUserData;
floorUserData->body = floorBody;
floorUserData->sprite = floorSprite;
floorUserData->fixtureType = FT_ROCK;
floorBody->SetUserData((void*)floorUserData);

// Ceiling
b2BodyDef ceilingBodyDef;
ceilingBodyDef.position.Set(800 * (offset + 1)
     / PTM_RATIO, screenSize.height / PTM_RATIO);
b2Body* ceilingBody = world->
     CreateBody(&ceilingBodyDef);
float angle = CC_DEGREES_TO_RADIANS(180);
b2Vec2 pos = ceilingBody->GetPosition();
ceilingBody->SetTransform(pos, angle);
GB2ShapeCache::sharedGB2ShapeCache()->
     addFixturesToBody(ceilingBody, "groundDirt");
Sprite* ceilingSprite =
Sprite::createWithSpriteFrameName("groundDirt.png");
ceilingSprite->setAnchorPoint(Point(0,0));
ceilingSprite->setPosition(Point(ceilingBody->
     GetPosition().x * PTM_RATIO, ceilingBody->
     GetPosition().y * PTM_RATIO));
ceilingSprite->setRotation(180);
this->addChild(ceilingSprite);
```

```
        ObstacleUserData* ceilingUserData =
                new ObstacleUserData;
        ceilingUserData->body = ceilingBody;
        ceilingUserData->sprite = ceilingSprite;
        ceilingUserData->fixtureType = FT_ROCK;
        ceilingBody->SetUserData((void*)ceilingUserData);
}
if(obstacleCounter >= kMaxObstaclePoints)
{
        return;
}
offsetEnd = offsetRock + quantity;
```

1. We create a Box2D body for the floor and we retrieve the fixture configuration file using the `GB2ShapeCache` class. The body is configured as static because we do not want that the gravity affects it
2. We configure the `ObstacleUserData` and we assign it to the body user data
3. We repeat the same process for the ceiling objects
4. We set the position of the body using an offset that increase automatically as more objects are added to the scene

Now we continue to by adding the obstacles and the pickups,

```
//Generate rocks and sensor
for(; offsetRock < offsetEnd; offsetRock++)
{
        // Upper rock
        b2BodyDef upperBodyDef;
        upperBodyDef.position.Set(obstaclePoints[offsetRock].x
                / PTM_RATIO, (screenSize.height -
                obstaclePoints[offsetRock].y + 50 )/ PTM_RATIO);
        b2Body* upperBody = world->CreateBody(&upperBodyDef);
        GB2ShapeCache::sharedGB2ShapeCache()->
                addFixturesToBody(upperBody, "rockDown");
        Sprite* upperSprite =
        Sprite::createWithSpriteFrameName("rockDown.png");
```

```
upperSprite->setAnchorPoint(Point(0,0));

upperSprite->setPosition(Point(
upperBody->GetPosition().x * PTM_RATIO,
upperBody->GetPosition().y * PTM_RATIO));
this->addChild(upperSprite, -1);

ObstacleUserData* upperUserData = new ObstacleUserData;
upperUserData->body = upperBody;
upperUserData->sprite = upperSprite;
upperUserData->fixtureType = FT_ROCK;
upperBody->SetUserData((void*)upperUserData);

// Down rock
b2BodyDef downBodyDef;
downBodyDef.position.Set(obstaclePoints[offsetRock].x
    / PTM_RATIO, (screenSize.height * 0.3 -
obstaclePoints[offsetRock].y )/ PTM_RATIO);
b2Body* downBody = world->CreateBody(&downBodyDef);
GB2ShapeCache::sharedGB2ShapeCache()->
    addFixturesToBody(downBody, "rock");
Sprite* downSprite =
    Sprite::createWithSpriteFrameName("rock.png");
downSprite->setAnchorPoint(Point(0,0));
downSprite->setPosition(Point(downBody->GetPosition().x
    * PTM_RATIO, downBody->GetPosition().y *
    PTM_RATIO));
this->addChild(downSprite, -1);

ObstacleUserData* downUserData  = new ObstacleUserData;
downUserData->body = downBody;
downUserData->sprite = downSprite;
downUserData->fixtureType = FT_ROCK;
downBody->SetUserData((void*)downUserData);

// Star sensor
b2BodyDef starBodyDef;
starBodyDef.type = b2_kinematicBody;
```

```
      starBodyDef.position.Set((obstaclePoints[offsetRock].x
            + 85) / PTM_RATIO, (screenSize.height * 1.85 - 2
            * obstaclePoints[offsetRock].y) /
            (2 * PTM_RATIO));
    b2Body* starBody = world->CreateBody(&starBodyDef);
    GB2ShapeCache::sharedGB2ShapeCache()->
            addFixturesToBody(starBody, "starGold");
    Sprite* starSprite =
    Sprite::createWithSpriteFrameName("starGold.png");
    starSprite->setAnchorPoint(Point(0,0));
    starSprite->setPosition(Point(starBody->GetPosition().x
      * PTM_RATIO, starBody->GetPosition().y * PTM_RATIO));
    this->addChild(starSprite);

      ObstacleUserData* starUserData = new ObstacleUserData;
      starUserData->body = starBody;
      starUserData->sprite = starSprite;
      starUserData->fixtureType = FT_PICKUP;
      starBody->SetUserData((void*)starUserData);
}
```

1. We create a Box2D body for the rocks and we retrieve the fixture configuration file using the GB2ShapeCache class. The body is configured as static because we do not want that the gravity affects it
2. We configure the ObstacleUserData and we assign it to the body user data
3. We repeat the same process for the pickups objects. The only difference is that the stars are configured as sensors
4. We set the position of the body using an offset that increase automatically as more objects are added to the scene

Let's continue now on creating the Obstacle Layer. Add the following code at the constructor of the class,

```
if(this->init())
{
      //Configure data members
      this->body = NULL;
```

```
auto screenSize = Director::getInstance()->
    getWinSize();
    offset = 0;
offsetRock = 0;
obstacleCounter = 0;
// Generate rock points

float x;
float y;

x = screenSize.width * 2;
y = screenSize.height * 0.5
+ (int)( ((double)rand() / RAND_MAX - 0.5)
* screenSize.height * 0.25);

obstaclePoints[0] = Point(x, y);

for (int i = 1; i < kMaxObstaclePoints; i++)
{
    x += (int)( ((double)rand() / RAND_MAX - 0.5 )
    * screenSize.width * 0.25 ) + screenSize.width
    * 0.5;
    y = screenSize.height * 0.5 + (int)(
    ((double)rand() / RAND_MAX - 0.5)
    * screenSize.height * 0.25);
    obstaclePoints[i] = Point(x, y);
}

// Generate obstacles
generateObstacle(3);
}
```

On the constructor what we created is an array with a random position for the obstacle. The `generateObstacle` uses this array to fix the location the objects. We generated also three objects that will be displayed as default.

The final step is to create the layer and to add to the `GameScene`. Add the following code at the create method on the `ObstacleLayer` file,

```
ObstacleLayer* layer = new ObstacleLayer(world);
return layer;
```

And the following code at the `init` method on the `GameScene` file

```
obstacleLayer = ObstacleLayer::create(world);
this->addChild(obstacleLayer);
```

If you build and run the application, you should see something like this,

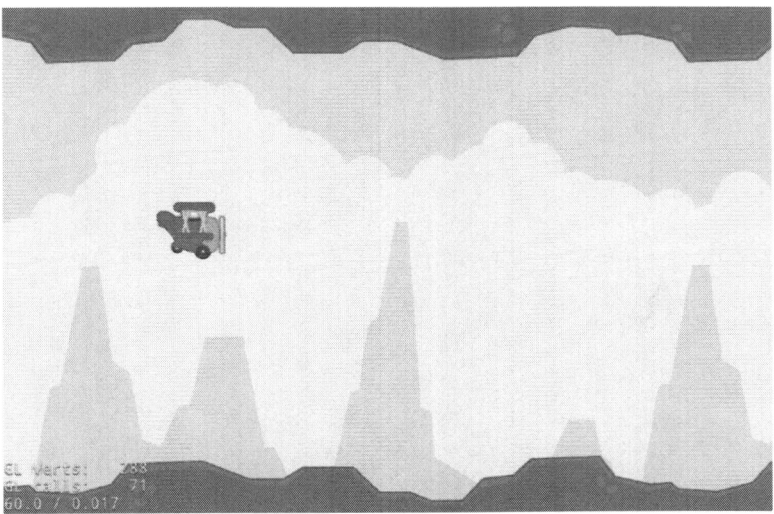

Scrolling Across the Map

After creating the game layout it is time to move the player across the screen. Performing this task is quite straightforward. Basically, you need to move the player and setup the position of the camera equal to the current position.

Let's add that code at the `update` method on the `GameScene.cpp` file,

```
// Update player position
auto screenSize = Director::getInstance()->getWinSize();
if(!impulseFlag)
{
```

```
    // Apply a constant force to the hero
    playerBody->ApplyLinearImpulse( b2Vec2(80,0),
      playerBody->GetWorldCenter(), true );
    impulseFlag = true;
}
// Move the layer at the same speed as the hero
b2Vec2 cameraCenterInPixels = PTM_RATIO * playerBody->
      GetPosition();
Point sceneOffset = Point(screenSize.width * 0.2
      - cameraCenterInPixels.x, screenSize.height * 0.5);
setPositionX(sceneOffset.x);
```

1. We apply only once an impulse to the `playerBody`. This is enough for our game since there is no force that will oppose to the movement of the plane
2. We calculate the next position of the camera considering the position of the body
3. We update the position of the Layer

Finally, add at the `init` method,

```
impulseFlag = false;
```

If you build and run the application you will notice that at some point there are no new elements in the scene. The reason is that we want to avoid allocating memory for objects that are not display in the screen.

Therefore, the next step will be to create and destroy objects, as the plane is moving across the screen. Add the following code right after the update of the layer's position

```
// Create and destroy objects
b2Body* bNext;
bool deleted = false;
for (b2Body* b = world->GetBodyList(); b; b = bNext)
{
    bNext = b->GetNext();
    b2Vec2 position = b->GetPosition();
    if (((position.x * PTM_RATIO + sceneOffset.x) <
```

```
        - screenSize.width) && b)
    {
        ObstacleUserData* fud = (ObstacleUserData*)b->
            GetUserData();
        obstacleLayer->removeChild(fud->sprite, true);
        world->DestroyBody(b);

        deleted = true;
    }
}
// If any element was deleted, generate more
if (deleted)
{
    obstacleLayer->generateObstacle(1);
    deleted = false;
}
```

1. We verify if the object is within a certain range of the scene. If this is the case we destroy both the Box2D object and Sprite
2. In the case that an object is deleted, we add a new object to the scene

If you build and run the application you will see as new objects are created as the plane move across the screen.

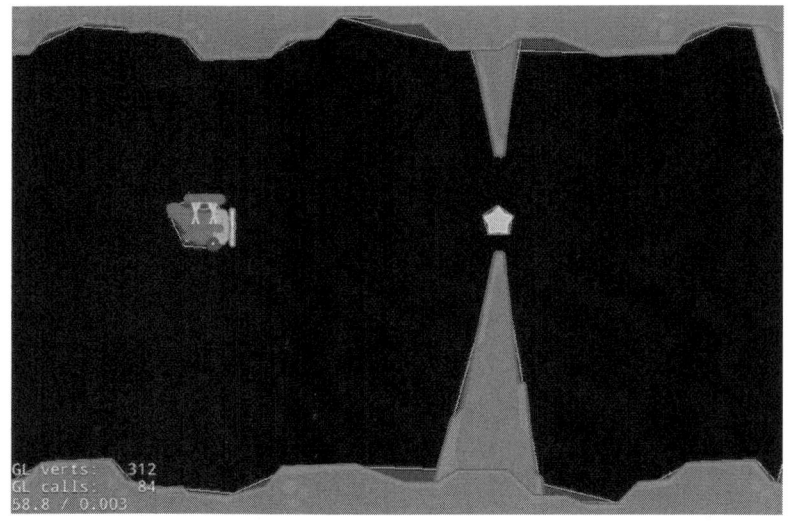

Now that we have some objects moving in the screen, we can complete the logic related with the collisions. Add the following code at the beginning of the update method on the GameScene.cpp file,

```
// Erase pickup
for (std::set<ObstacleUserData*>::iterator it
        = m_pickupsToProcess.begin();
        it != m_pickupsToProcess.end(); ++it)
{
        ObstacleUserData* fud = *it;
        obstacleLayer->removeChild(fud->sprite, true);
        world->DestroyBody(fud->body);
        m_pickupsToProcess.erase(it);

        break;
}
```

And the following one at the BeginContact on the GameSceneContactListener class,

```
// Player hit a pick up

if ( fudA && fudA->fixtureType == FT_PICKUP && fB->GetBody()
```

```
       == layer->getPlayerBody() )
{
    layer->m_pickupsToProcess.insert(fudA);
}
if ( fudB && fudB->fixtureType == FT_PICKUP && fA->GetBody()
       == layer->getPlayerBody() )
{
    layer->m_pickupsToProcess.insert(fudB);
}
```

1. At the contact listener each time that there is a collision between the plane and a pickup, we insert the pickup object in the m_pickupsToProcess set

2. At each game's iteration, we verify the m_pickupsToProcess set. If there is an object we destroy both the sprite and the Box2D object

To finish, we add the logic associated with the collision between the plane and the rocks. At the init method of the GameScene.cpp file add,

```
gameOverFlag = false;
```

Then, at the update method just right before the step of the Box2D world,

```
if(gameOverFlag)
{
        return;
}
```

And finally, at the BeginContact on the GameSceneContactListener class the following code,

```
if ( fudA && fudA->fixtureType == FT_ROCK && fB->GetBody()
       == layer->getPlayerBody() )
{
    layer->setGameOverFlag(true);
}
if ( fudB && fudB->fixtureType == FT_ROCK && fA->GetBody()
       == layer->getPlayerBody() )
```

```
{
    layer->setGameOverFlag(true);
}
```

Basically, we stop the simulation of the Box2D after the plane collides with a rock. Additional logic could be added to display a Game-Over screen with the final score achieved.

Adding Parallax Effect

Parallax effect is a technique in which the background images move by the camera slower than the foreground images, creating an illusion of depth and adding to the immersion.

Cocos2d-x offers such feature with the class `ParallaxNode`. However, by default this class does not provide infinite scroll. Luckily, a guy called Aram Kocharyan created the library Parallax Scrolling, which allows user to make an infinite parallax effect on cocos2d quite straightforward. The original code was ported to cocos2d-x by Jason Marziani and adapted to cocos2d-x 3.x by Stefan Nguyen.

Using the Parallax Scrolling library is quite simple. Open the file `BackgroundGameLayer.cpp` and add the following code at the `init` method,

```
parallax = CCParallaxScrollNode::create();
auto bg1 = Sprite::createWithSpriteFrameName
        ("GameBackground.png");
auto bg2 = Sprite::createWithSpriteFrameName
        ("GameBackground.png");
parallax->addInfiniteScrollXWithZ(-1,Point(0.1,0.1),
        Point(0, 0), bg1, bg2, NULL);
this->addChild(parallax);
//create main loop
scheduleUpdate();
```

1. We create the `CCParallaxScrollNode`
2. We add the sprites that compose the parallax effect
3. We configure the infinite scrolling by setting the depth, the ratio, the position and sprites
4. We add the parallax effect as a child to the layer

To animate the parallax effect it is enough to add the following line at the update method

```
parallax->updateWithVelocity(Point(-10,0), dt);
```

Now, let's include the background layer to the game scene. Open the `GameScen.cpp` file, and add the following line of code to the scene `method`,

```
scene->addChild(layer->setupBackgroundLayer(), -1);
```

If you build and run the application you will see that the parallax effects in the Game Scene.

Summary

In this chapter you learned how to create a game layout by using both code and supporting tools. You also learned how to scroll across the layout and how to add parallax effect to background layers. Additional elements to the game logic were added to the application.

Sound Effects and Music

This chapter provides a description on how to include sound effects and music into your games. You will learn how to use the sound engine provided by Cocos2d-x and how to add audio into your application.

Go ahead and download the chapter files from https://github.com/DragonBackGames/BookCocos2DX/tree/master/CHAPTER_9. This folder contains a basic project with a template to work along this chapter.

Introduction to SimpleAudioEngine

Cocos2d-x provides a sound engine through `SimpleAudioEngine`. This component is a wrapper that simplifies the usage of audio files cross platforms. By using this engine, the user can play one background music and multiple sound effects synchronously. The formats supported depends on the platforms,

Background Music

Platform	Format
Android	Supports the formats as android.media.MediaPlayer
iOS	Supports the formats as CocosDenshion
Windows	Supports MID and WAV, but it does not support MP3
Marmalade	Supports MP3
Blackberry	Supports OGG

Sound Effects

Platform	Format
Android	Best support for OGG
iOS	Supports the formats as CocosDenshion
Windows	Supports MID and WAV
Marmalade	Only support PCM
Blackberry	Supports WAV

Adding Sound Effects and Music

Using the `SimpleAudioEngine` is quite straightforward. Open the `AppDelegate.cpp` file and add the following code at the `applicationDidFinishLaunching` methods,

```
...
// turn on display FPS
director->setDisplayStats(true);

// Start music
CocosDenshion::SimpleAudioEngine::getInstance()->
        playBackgroundMusic("music.mp3");
...
```

Let's continue by adding some sound effects. Open the `GameScene.cpp` file at the `onTouchBegan` method,

```
CocosDenshion::SimpleAudioEngine::getInstance()->
      playEffect("jump.wav");
```

And the following at the `GameSceneContactListener::BeginContact` method,

```
// Player hit a pick up
if ( fudA && fudA->fixtureType == FT_PICKUP && fB->GetBody()
      == layer->getPlayerBody() )
{
    layer->m_pickupsToProcess.insert(fudA);
    // Play effect
    CocosDenshion::SimpleAudioEngine::getInstance()->
          playEffect("pickup.wav");
}
if ( fudB && fudB->fixtureType == FT_PICKUP && fA->GetBody()
      == layer->getPlayerBody() )
{
    layer->m_pickupsToProcess.insert(fudB);
```

```
    // Play effect
    CocosDenshion::SimpleAudioEngine::getInstance()->
        playEffect("pickup.wav");
}

// Player hit a rock
if ( fudA && fudA->fixtureType == FT_ROCK && fB->GetBody()
        == layer->getPlayerBody() )
{
    layer->setGameOverFlag(true);
    // Play effect
    CocosDenshion::SimpleAudioEngine::getInstance()->
        playEffect("hit.wav");
}
if ( fudB && fudB->fixtureType == FT_ROCK && fA->GetBody()
        == layer->getPlayerBody() )
{
    layer->setGameOverFlag(true);
    // Play effect
    CocosDenshion::SimpleAudioEngine::getInstance()->
        playEffect("hit.wav");
}
```

1. We used the audio engine to load and play the background music
2. We use the audio engine to load and play a sound effect when the plane jumps, grabs a pickup or collides with an obstacle

If you build and run the application you hear the background music playing in loop and the sound effects each time that there is an event.

Controlling Volume

The sound engine also offers the possibility to control the music and sound effects by pausing, resuming and setting the volume.

Open once again the `AppDelegate.cpp` file and add the following code at the `applicationDidEnterBackground` method,

```
CocosDenshion::SimpleAudioEngine::getInstance()->
    pauseAllEffects();
CocosDenshion::SimpleAudioEngine::getInstance()->
    pauseBackgroundMusic();
```

And the following one at the `applicationWillEnterForeground` method,

```
CocosDenshion::SimpleAudioEngine::getInstance()->
    resumeAllEffects();
CocosDenshion::SimpleAudioEngine::getInstance()->
    resumeBackgroundMusic();
```

1. We tell to the sound engine to pause the background music and sound effects in case that the application goes inactive
2. We tell to the sound engine to resume the background music and sound effects in case the application goes active again

Beside pausing and resuming the audio, you have also the possibility to control the volume of both the background music and the sound effects. Open the `SettingsScene.cpp` file and add the following code at the `clickSoundButton` method,

```
if(effectFlag)
{
    CocosDenshion::SimpleAudioEngine::getInstance()->
        setEffectsVolume(0.0);
    effectFlag = false;
}
else
{
    CocosDenshion::SimpleAudioEngine::getInstance()->
        setEffectsVolume(1.0);
    effectFlag = true;
}
```

And the following to the `clickMusicButtun` method,

```
if(musicFlag)
{
    CocosDenshion::SimpleAudioEngine::getInstance()->
        setBackgroundMusicVolume(0.0);
    musicFlag = false;
}
else
{
    CocosDenshion::SimpleAudioEngine::getInstance()->
        setBackgroundMusicVolume(1.0);
    musicFlag = true;
}
```

Both the sound and music buttons are configured as toggle buttons. When one of these buttons is pressed the volume will be set to 0 or to 1 depending on the previous state.

If you build and run the application you will notice how the volume of the background music and sound effects changes while pressing the buttons at the Settings Scene.

Summary

In this chapter you learned how to use the audio engine provided by Cocos2d-x to use audio files within your game. You learn how to load and play background music and sound effects. Finally, you learn how to pause, resume and control the volume of the audio files. Next step would be to load different kinds of background music while changing scene or handling events such as Game Over.

Saving Game Data

This chapter describes how to save your game data in your application. The idea is to enable the user to store data such as high score, user preferences, game progression and many others. Here it is described two methods that could be used for such purpose, store user default data and SQLite3.

Go ahead and download the chapter files from https://github.com/DragonBackGames/BookCocos2DX/tree/master/CHAPTER_10 This folder contains a basic project with a template to work along this chapter.

Using User Default Data

In some cases you need to store small amount of data relative to your application. For this purpose, Cocos2d-x offers the object `UserDefault`. This objects store data in a default file. There are five possible types of data that you can access: integers, floats, double, boolean and strings.

Open the file `ForegroundGameLayer.cpp` and add the following code at the end of the `init` method,

```
// Initialize score
scorePoints = 0;
bestPoints = UserDefault::getInstance()->
        getIntegerForKey("score", 0);
```

With this method, we load the best score with a default value equal to zero. Now, add to the following code at the `setGameOverSplash` method in the same file,

```
// Save best score with store data
if (bestPoints < scorePoints)
{
        bestPoints = scorePoints;
```

```
}
UserDefault::getInstance()->
      setIntegerForKey("score", bestPoints);
```

Here we set the value of best score in the configuration file.

You can store as many values you want for your application. If you build and run the application you will notice how the high score is saved while playing again or reopening the application.

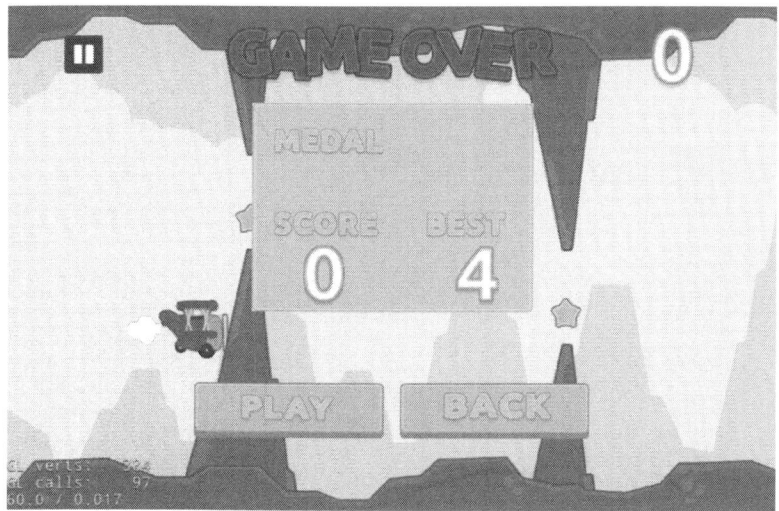

Using SQLite3

SQLite is a software library that implements a self-contained, serverless, zero-configuration, transactional SQL database engine.

Using SQLite within Cocos2d-x is quite simple. Basically, you need to add the sqlite3 files into your project and access to the database using the API offered by the library. In order to manipulate user files such as a database, Cocos2d-x offers the object `FileUtils`.

To access the database file you can use the following code,

```
std::string dbPath = FileUtils::getInstance()->
      fullPathForFilename("database.db3");
#if CC_TARGET_PLATFORM == CC_PLATFORM_ANDROID
      dbPath  = FileUtils::getInstance()->
            getWritablePath();
      dbPath  += "/save.db3";
      FILE* file = fopen(dbPath.c_str(), "r");
      if (file == nullptr)
      {
            unsigned long size;
            const char* data =
            (char*) FileUtils::getInstance()->
                  getFileData("dict.db", "rb", &size);
            file = fopen(dbPath.c_str(), "wb");
            fwrite(data, size, 1, file);
            CC_SAFE_DELETE_ARRAY(data);
      }
        fclose(file);
#endif
```

The SQLite library provides a set of API that allows the user to input commands required for manipulating the database. The most relevant commands used on SQLite3 are the following,

Create new table example

```
CREATE  TABLE  users  (id  INTEGER  PRIMARY  KEY,login
TEXT,pass TEXT);
```

The 'id' column is here what you call autoincrement in MySQL.

Valid column types,

- TEXT
- INTEGER
- REAL

- BLOB

Rename table example

```
ALTER TABLE users RENAME TO client_users
```

This renames table users to `client_users`

SELECT example

```
SELECT * FROM table_name WHERE column_name = value
```

Selects all rows in table `table_name` where column `column_name` is equal to value

UPDATE example

```
UPDATE table_name SET column_name = update_value
WHERE some_column = some_value
```

Updates `column_name` with the value `update_value` in table `table_name`, on row/s where `some_column` is equal to `some_value`

DELETE example

```
DELETE FROM table_name WHERE column_name < 4
```

Deletes all rows from `table_name` where `column_name` is less than 4

INSERT example

```
INSERT INTO table_name (column1, column4, column7)
VALUES (value1, 'value2', value3)
```

Inserts a new row into table `table_name` with values value1 in column1, value2 in column4 and value3 in column7 (other columns in table are left null or with default values, if set).

Summary

In this chapter you learned how to save user data for your games in Cocos2d-x. You learn how to user default object to store simple data in a default file. Also, you saw some principles on how to use SQLite3 within your application.

Made in the USA
San Bernardino, CA
25 November 2014